MW01628311

D.C. Daniel–
Washington Superhero

Dream!
Sue Pyatt

To Jennifer, Laura, Dana, Everett, Laurie, Jeff, Erica, and Emmie

First Edition

ISBN 9780974257525

Printed in the United States of America

IMAGINATION STATION PRESS
–a subsidiary of Snowspring Ltd.
Arlington, Virginia

D.C. DANIEL – WASHINGTON SUPERHERO

Story by
Sue Pyatt
Illustrated by
Dana Saxerud

Why am I a Superhero at age eight?
Well, I guess you'd have to call it fate.

One day, I heard a scary sound.
Suddenly my heart began to pound.

A robber crashed out of a candy store
With a wad of bucks plus treats galore.

Wow, was this guy a nervous wreck!
He slipped on a bill and hit the deck.

DO NOT TRY THIS AT HOME!

Before he could get off the ground,
I grabbed his bag and spun around.

Racing to the corner with fast feet,
I spied a manhole cover in the street.

When the man came charging after me,
He plunged in the hole and hurt his knee.

I heard him sobbing, "Oh my knee!
That rotten kid has caused an injury."

Looking for a place to disappear,
I ran to a ballpark that was near.

At the park I ran to Dragon Creech,
And begged, “Hide me out of reach!”

The robber scoured the entire space,
But he couldn't find my hiding place.

CAN YOU?

Next I shot to the Metro with such zip,
That I'm still amazed I didn't trip.

Leaping on a Green train just in time,
I then transferred to the Orange Line.

The Smithsonian was a crowded place,
So I thought he might give up the chase.

Not him. The guy was crazy mad.
He wanted the money really bad.

As I neared the Castle, I could see
That robber was still chasing me.

But he was behind and panting.
"I'll get you!" He yelled ranting.

Smithsonian National Museum of American History
ME
At American History,
This wasn't a game,
As I dived behind
An old steam engine train.

He almost caught up at Air and Space.
But I lost him and kept up the chase.

N-X-211
RYAN
Spirit of St. Louis
USAF
IMA
APOLLO 11

On to Natural History, where
I hid beside a T-Rex there.

Outside he couldn't outrun me at all,
So he snatched a scooter off the mall.

At Washington Monument, I was silly
As I wove the flagpoles willy-nilly.

Near the White House, low in the sky,
The President landed as I raced by.

At this point, I was feeling tired
And, from stress, a little wired.

Suddenly a building site appeared.
I saw a tiny fence hole, as I neared.

Up, up, up I climbed on a huge backhoe.
The robber looked so little down below.

Showing he lacked common sense,
He tried to follow through the fence.

Yeah sure, he was still on my case.
But for a while, I slowed his pace.

Caught in wire he couldn't break,
I yelled, "You made a big mistake!"

To Lincoln Memorial I made a dash
Still holding on to treats and cash.

The guy was again in hot pursuit.
Oh how he wanted back his loot.

At the boathouse, I squeaked with urgency,
"Please, lend me a canoe. It's an emergency!"

Before the boatman said, "What for?"
I grabbed a red canoe and then an oar.

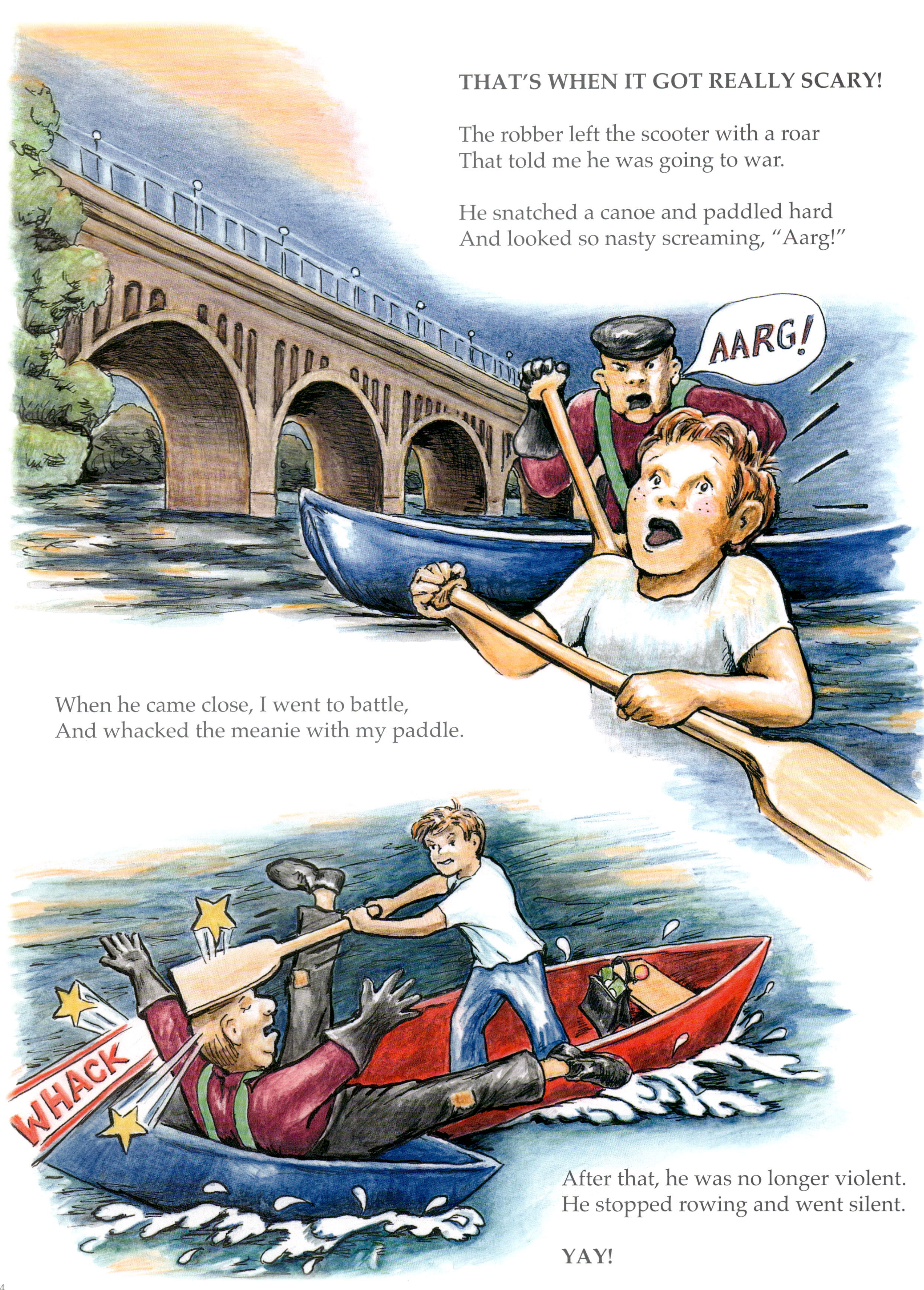

THAT'S WHEN IT GOT REALLY SCARY!

The robber left the scooter with a roar
That told me he was going to war.

He snatched a canoe and paddled hard
And looked so nasty screaming, "Aarg!"

When he came close, I went to battle,
And whacked the meanie with my paddle.

After that, he was no longer violent.
He stopped rowing and went silent.

YAY!

I rowed my canoe back immediately
And shrieked, “A bad man is after me!”
BOAT RENTAL
KENNEDY CENTER
911 HELP POLICE!
Uh-oh, the evil guy suddenly re-appeared.
“I got you now Mr. Smarty!” He sneered.
I saw his face was a terrible, angry red.
Oh man! A big bump was on his head.

Just when I thought there was no hope,
A police helicopter dropped a rope.

Grabbing the rope, up in the air I soared.
The robber stared and looked quite floored.

Then, the police nabbed the bad guy quickly.
In handcuffs, Mr. Nasty looked so sickly.

Want to know what was extremely fun?
Returning that money was how I WON.

When I got home, my Mom said, “Whew!
Daniel, you have some explaining to do.”

“Talk Daniel.” Her voice was very loud.
I said, “Okay Mom, you’ll be so proud.”

I took her for a walk, told all the action,
And explained the story to her satisfaction.

Here I am with the Mayor of D.C.
Receiving the Medal for Bravery.

Don't mess with me, or I'll go KERPOW!
Bad guys beware! I'm a Superhero now.

THE END

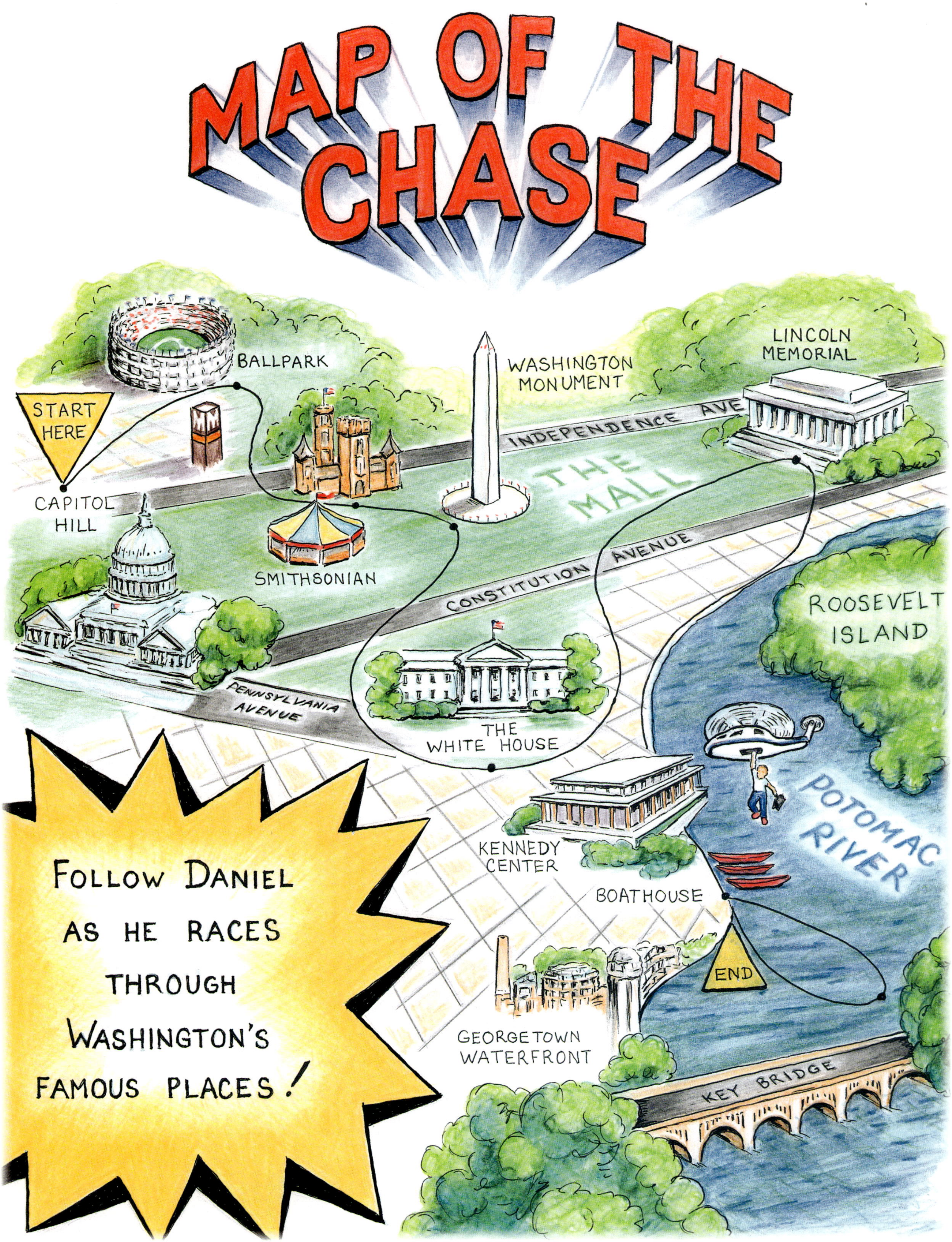

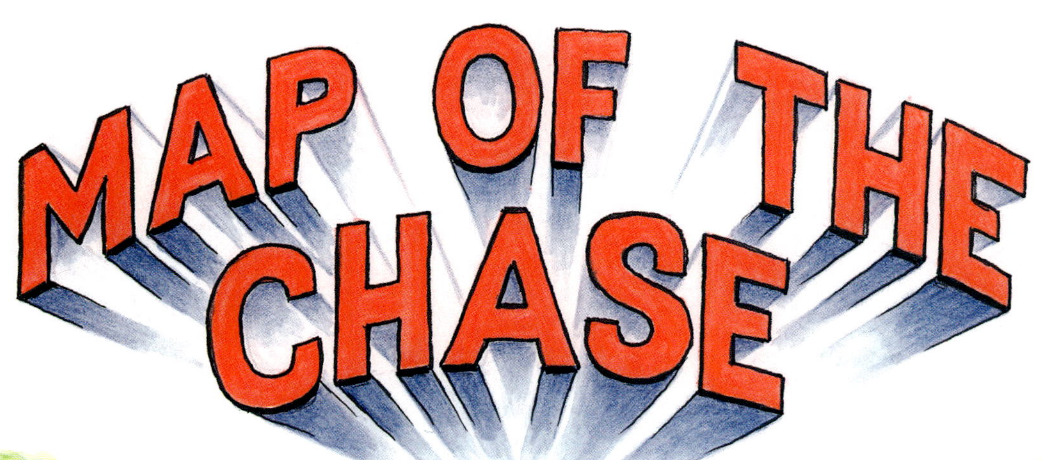

MAP OF THE CHASE
START HERE
BALLPARK
WASHINGTON MONUMENT
LINCOLN MEMORIAL
INDEPENDENCE AVE
CAPITOL HILL
THE MALL
SMITHSONIAN
CONSTITUTION AVENUE
ROOSEVELT ISLAND
PENNSYLVANIA AVENUE
THE WHITE HOUSE
POTOMAC RIVER
KENNEDY CENTER
BOATHOUSE
END
GEORGETOWN WATERFRONT
KEY BRIDGE
FOLLOW DANIEL AS HE RACES THROUGH WASHINGTON'S FAMOUS PLACES!